Michael M. Dediu

Bureaucracy is growing like a weed – People Want a Quality Change

Yup, that's right! Better life for all!

DERC Publishing House

Nashua, New Hampshire, U. S. A.

Copyright ©2021   by Michael M. Dediu

Published and printed in the
United States of America
On the Great Seal of the United States are included:
E Pluribus Unum (Out of many, one)
Annuit Coeptis (He has approved of the undertakings)
Novus Ordo Seclorum (New order of the ages)

Library of Congress Control Number: 2021907174

Dediu, Michael M.

Bureaucracy is growing like a weed – People Want a Quality
Change
Yup, that's right! Better life for all!

ISBN-13: 978-1-950999-36-1

1-10381969331
1-4RP7RA4
00130D
26RSD90O
1-4RP7GX0

Preface

Around 1795, George Washington wrote: "Government is not reason; it is not eloquent; it is force. Like fire, it is a dangerous servant, and a fearful master."

After thousands of years of such governments all over the place, obviously the bureaucracy is growing like a weed, and the people want a quality change really fast - no bureaucracy whatsoever!

The over 7.7 billions of people on Earth impatiently ask for a friendly, helpful, compassionate, polite, prompt and smart World Government, with no bureaucracy!

This book is exactly about a quality change to a much better and non-bureaucratic world management, with clear, short and practical ideas.

Bottom Line: Eliminate bureaucracy and keep it away!

Michael M. Dediu, Ph. D.

Nashua, New Hampshire, U. S. A., 19 April 2021

USA, Bristol, allegoric sculpture at Linden Place (1810, home of the DeWolfs and the Colts, with Bristol Art Museum (1963, left back) on Wardwell Street near Hope Street, located in the Ballroom of the Linden Place.

Table of Contents

Italy, Rome (753 BC, one of the oldest cities in Europe, called Roma Aeterna (The Eternal City) and Caput Mundi (Capital of the World)), from the Pincian Hill looking southwest: Piazza del Popolo (1822), with the Egyptian obelisk (36 m) of Sety I (1290–1279 BC) and Rameses II (1303, 1279–1213 BC) from Heliopolis, brought in 10 BC by Augustus (63 BC-14 AD) for Circus Maximus, in 1589 here. Basilica San Pietro (1506, 132 m, back).

1 – We all know - World is a family of 7.7 Billions

Having a family of over 7.7 billions of people on our Earth, it is only natural to have an adequate administrative management of this huge family, without bureaucracy. We will present a general view about this management, which has to be friendly, helpful, fast, polite, modest and very smart.

Impossible? No!

Inevitable? Of course!

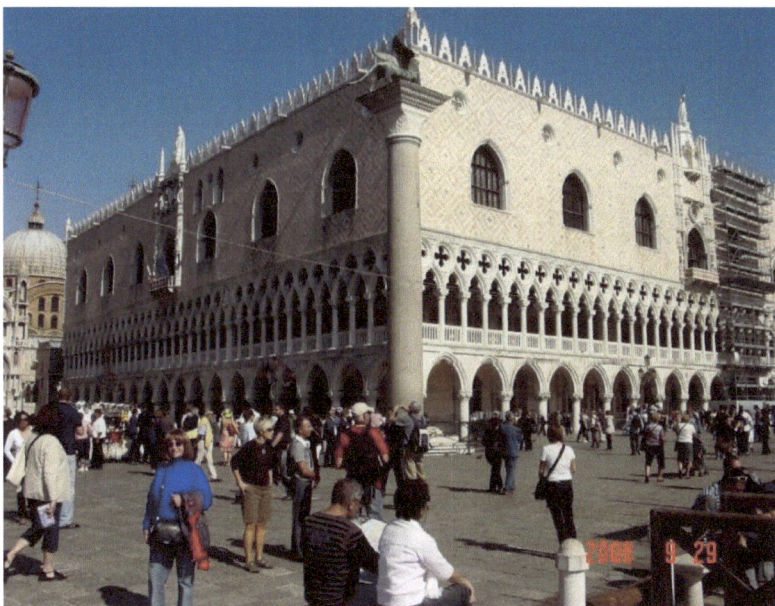

29 Sep 2008, Piazza San Marco (1084) looking northeast, Palazzo Ducale (1424), Basilica di San Marco (1173, left back). Column of the Lion (center, with the sculpture Lion of Venice on top), Italy.

1.1. 10 Simple Regions with 770 M people each

The new 10 regions, each with about 770 M people, called R0, R1,…, R9, should be delimited by meridians (or line of longitudes), with the assistance of the United Nations, each region having a pair of capitals (which will change every year), for example:

R0 between meridians 0 and 15^0 E, capitals: Bern and Libreville (Gabon) – assistance from Oxford (UK). For better quality and consistency of the management, we'll have the first two cities from the region R0, and the third city from outside. Actually, being inside the same country Terra, any city, sub-region or region can ask for advice or help from anybody.

R1: 15^0 E - 30^0 E, Warsaw (Poland) and Pretoria (South Africa) – assistance from Miami (FL, USA).

R2: 30^0 E - 45^0 E, Moscow and Cairo – assistance from Grenoble (France).

R3: 45^0 E - 75^0 E, Astana (Kazakhstan) and Karachi (Pakistan) – assistance from Montpellier (France).

R4: 75^0 E - 85^0 E, New Delhi (India) and Novosibirsk (Russia) – assistance from Magdeburg (Germany).

R5: 85^0 E - 100^0 E, Krasnoyarsk (Russia) and Urumqi (China) – assistance from Avignon (France)

R6: 100^0 E - 115^0 E Jakarta (Indonesia) and Beijing – assistance from Neuchâtel (Switzerland).

R7: 115^0 E - 180^0, Tokyo and Sydney (Australia) – assistance from Malmö (Sweden).

R8: 180^0 - 70^0 W, Washington and Mexico City – assistance from Bellinzona (Switzerland).

R9: 70^0 W – 0, Halifax (Canada) and Brasilia – assistance from Biel (Switzerland).

1.2. 100 Sub-regions with 77 M people each

Each of the 10 regions from 1.1 above will be divided by meridians in 10 sub-regions R00,   , R99, each with about 77 M people, and no bureaucracy.

The Rainbow Bridge between Canada (left) and USA (right), crosses Niagara River, 500 m north-west from the American Falls, opened 1941, longest span 298 m, seen from the Prospect Point Observation Tower (70 m north of the American Falls).

In Region R0: from Paris (France) to N'Djamena (Chad)

- The sub-region R00 will have the capitals Paris (France) and Niamey (Niger) – assistance from Magdeburg (Germany).
- The sub-region R01 will have the capitals Brussels (Belgium) and Porto-Novo (Benin) - assistance from Toronto (Canada).
- The sub-region R02 will have the capitals Amsterdam (Netherlands) and Algiers (Algeria) - assistance from Graz (Austria).
- The sub-region R03 will have the capitals Luxembourg (Luxembourg) and Sao Tome (Sao Tome and Principe) - assistance from Adelaide (Australia).
- The sub-region R04 will have the capitals of Abuja (Nigeria) and Bochum (Germany) - assistance from Nikko (Japan).
- The sub-region R05 will have the capitals Malabo (Equatorial Guinea), Zürich (Switzerland) - assistance from Leeds (UK).
- The sub-region R06 will have the capitals Oslo (Norway) and Tunis (Tunisia) - assistance from Sheffield (UK).
- The sub-region R07 will have the capitals Roma (Italy) and Luanda (Angola) - assistance from Yamagata (Japan).
- The sub-region R08 will have the capitals in Berlin (Germany) and Tripoli (Libya) - assistance from New York (USA).
- The sub-region R09 will have the capitals Prague (Czech Republic) and N'Djamena (Chad) - assistance from Brisbane (Australia).

26 Nov 2008, Shinjuku Center Building (223 m, 54 fl, 1979, center), Mode Gakuen Cocoon Tower (204 m, 50 fl, 2008, center-right), Keio Plaza Hotel North Tower (180 m, 47 fl, 1971, right).

In Region R1: from Zagreb (Croatia) to Bujumbura (Burundi)

- The sub-region R10 will have the capitals in Zagreb (Croatia) and Brazzaville (Congo) - assistance from Nantes (France).
- The sub-region R11 will have the capitals in Vienna (Austria), Windhoek (Namibia) - assistance from Bilbao (Spain).
- The sub-region R12 will have the capitals in Stockholm (Sweden), Bangui (Central African Republic) - assistance from Florence (Italy).
- The sub-region R13 will have the capitals in Budapest (Hungary), Rundu (Namibia) - assistance from Monaco (Monaco).
- The sub-region R14 will have the capitals in Belgrade (Serbia), Kananga (Democratic Republic of Congo) - assistance from Liverpool (UK).
- The sub-region R15 will have the capitals in Athens (Greece), Mongu (Zambia) - assistance from Los Angeles (CA, USA).
- The sub-region R16 will have the capitals in Helsinki (Finland) and Gaborone (Botswana) - assistance from Montreal (Canada).
- The sub-region R17 will have the capitals in Bucharest (Romania) and Gaborone (Botswana) - assistance from Philadelphia (PA, USA).
- The sub-region R18 will have the capitals in Minsk (Belarus) and Maseru (Lesotho) - assistance from Orleans (France).
- The sub-region R19 will have the capitals in Chisinau (Republic of Moldova) and Bujumbura (Burundi) - assistance from Hamburg (Germany).

USA, Chicago 1837: Willoughby Tower (1929, 38 fl, 134 m, right), Chicago Athletic Association Bldg., Anno Domini 1891, center

In Region R2: from Kiev (Ukraine) to Baghdad (Iraq)

- The sub-region R20 will have the capitals in Kiev (Ukraine) and Kigali (Rwanda) - assistance from Ottawa (Canada).
- The sub-region R21 will have the capitals in Ankara (Turkey) and Khartoum (Sudan) - assistance from Salzburg (Austria).
- The sub-region R22 will have the capitals in Lilongwe (Malawi) and Nicosia (Cyprus) - assistance from Dallas (TX, USA).
- The sub-region R23 will have the capitals in Jerusalem (Israel) and Dodoma (Tanzania) - assistance from Strasbourg (France).
- The sub-region R24 will have the capitals in Damascus (Syria) and Nairobi (Kenya) - assistance from Stuttgart (Germany).
- The sub-region R25 will have the capitals in Krasnodar (Russia) and Addis Ababa (Ethiopia) - assistance from Marseille (France).
- The sub-region R26 will have the capitals in Rostov-on-Don (Russia) and Asmara (Eritrea) - assistance from Leipzig (Germany).
- The sub-region R27 will have the capitals in Stavropol (Russia) and Djibouti (Djibouti) - assistance from Zürich (Switzerland).
- The sub-region R28 will have the capitals in Mosul (Iraq) and Moroni (Comoros) - assistance from Linz (Austria).
- The sub-region R29 will have the capitals in Yerevan (Armenia) and Baghdad (Iraq) - assistance from Göttingen (Germany).

6 April 1978, Pisa, Cattedrale di Pisa (1092, striped-marble, left), Torre di Pisa (August 1173-1372, 55.86 m on the low side, 56.67 m on the high side, white-marble, 296 steps, right).

In Region R3: from Riyadh (Saudi Arabia) to Malé (Maldives)

- The sub-region R30 will have the capitals in Riyadh (Saudi Arabia) and Mogadishu (Somalia) - assistance from Bonn (Germany).
- The sub-region R31 will have the capitals in Baku (Azerbaijan) and Antananarivo (Madagascar) - assistance from Le Mans (France).
- The sub-region R32 will have the capitals in Oral (Kazakhstan) and Tehran (Iran) - assistance from Pisa (Italy).
- The sub-region R33 will have the capitals in Ashgabat (Turkmenistan) and Abu Dhabi (United Arab Emirates) - assistance from Wolfsburg (Germany).
- The sub-region R34 will have the capitals in Magnitogorsk (Russia) and Muscat (Oman) - assistance from Toulouse (France).
- The sub-region R35 will have the capitals in Chelyabinsk (Russia) and Herat (Afghanistan) - assistance from Basel (Switzerland).
- The sub-region R36 will have the capitals in Tyumen (Russia) and Kandahar (Afghanistan) - assistance from Nagoya (Japan).
- The sub-region R37 will have the capitals in Dushanbe (Tajikistan) and Labytnangi (Russia) - assistance from Limoges (France).
- The sub-region R38 will have the capitals in Astana (Kazakhstan) and Kabul (Afghanistan) - assistance from Rostock (Germany).
- The sub-region R39 will have the capitals in Islamabad (Pakistan) and Malé (Maldives) - assistance from La Rochelle (France).

Japan: Mount Fuji (3,776 m, 1707 last eruption), seen from 17 km north in Kawaguchiko (Lake Kawaguchi, 6 km^2, 830 m elevation).

In Region R4: from Bishkek (Kyrgyzstan) to Brahmapur (India)

- The sub-region R40 will have the capitals in Bishkek (Kyrgyzstan) and Jaipur (India) - assistance from Osaka (Japan).
- The sub-region R41 will have the capitals in Akola (India) and Kashgar (China) - assistance from Genoa (Italy).
- The sub-region R42 will have the capitals in Almaty (Kazakhstan) and Coimbatore (India) - assistance from Perth (Australia).
- The sub-region R43 will have the capitals in Kuybyshev (Russia) and Agra (India) - assistance from Fukuoka (Japan).
- The sub-region R44 will have the capitals in Vertikos (Russia) and Nagpur (India) - assistance from Coral Bay (Australia).
- The sub-region R45 will have the capitals in Chennai (India) and Colombo (Sri Lanka) - assistance from Sapporo (Japan).
- The sub-region R46 will have the capitals in Lucknow (India) and Fedosikha (Russia) - assistance from Niigata (Japan).
- The sub-region R47 will have the capitals in Bilaspur (India) and Kolpashevo (Russia) - assistance from Albany (Australia).
- The sub-region R48 will have the capitals in Visakhapatnam (India) and Barnaul (Russia) - assistance from Hiroshima (Japan).
- The sub-region R49 will have the capitals in Brahmapur (India) and Tomsk (Russia) - assistance from Yokohama (Japan).

In Region R5: from Kathmandu (Nepal) to Dehong (China)
- The sub-region R50 will have the capitals in Kathmandu (Nepal) and Patna (India) - assistance from Kobe (Japan).
- The sub-region R51 will have the capitals in Bayingol (China) and Novokuznetsk (Russia) - assistance from Vichy (France).
- The sub-region R52 will have the capitals in Thimphu (Bhutan) and Dhaka (Bangladesh) - assistance from Jena (Germany).
- The sub-region R53 will have the capitals in Lhasa (China) and Achinsk (Russia) - assistance from Reims (France).
- The sub-region R54 will have the capitals in Abakan (Russia) and Kumul (China) - assistance from Fribourg (Switzerland).
- The sub-region R55 will have the capitals in Kyzyl (Russia) and Dibrugarh (India) - assistance from Denmark (Australia).
- The sub-region R56 will have the capitals in Bassein (Myanmar) and Tinsukia (India) - assistance from Chiba (Japan).

- The sub-region R57 will have the capitals in Yushu City (China) and Tinskoy (Russia) - assistance from Klagenfurt (Austria).
- The sub-region R58 will have the capitals in Jiuquan (China) and Medan (Indonesia) - assistance from Lucerne (Switzerland).
- The sub-region R59 will have the capitals in Chiang Mai (Thailand) and Dehong (China) - assistance from Mulhouse (France).

Canada, Niagara Falls: the American Falls (21-30 m drop, 290 m wide), the Bridal Veil Falls (right, 21m), after Luna Island

In Region R6: from Bangkok (Thailand) to Chita (Russia)

- The sub-region R60 will have the capitals in Bangkok (Thailand) and Kuala Lumpur (Malaysia) - assistance from Besançon (France).
- The sub-region R61 will have the capitals in Vientiane (Laos) and Singapore – assistance from Freiburg im Breisgau (Germany).
- The sub-region R62 will have the capitals in Phnom Penh (Cambodia) and Irkutsk (Russia) – assistance from Baden (Switzerland).
- The sub-region R63 will have the capitals in Palembang (Indonesia), Hanoi (Vietnam) – assistance from Thun (Switzerland).
- The sub-region R64 will have the capitals in Ulan Bator (Mongolia) and Ulan-Ude (Russia) – assistance from Chaumont (France).
- The sub-region R65 will have the capitals in Cirebon (Indonesia) and Nanning (China) – assistance from Vaduz (Lichtenstein).
- The sub-region R66 will have the capitals in Pontianak (Indonesia) and Baotou (China) – assistance from Lugano (Switzerland).
- The sub-region R67 will have the capitals in Surakarta (Indonesia) and Yichang (China) – assistance from Thonon-les-Bain (France).
- The sub-region R68 will have the capitals in Surabaya (Indonesia) and Changsha (China) – assistance from Burgdorf (Switzerland).
- The sub-region R69 will have the capitals in Chita (Russia) and Hong Kong (China) – assistance from Colmar (France).

In Region R7: from Nanchang (China) to Melbourne (Australia)

- The sub-region R70 will have the capitals in Bandar Seri Begawan (Brunei Darussalam) and Nanchang (China) – assistance from Turku (Finland).
- The sub-region R71 will have the capitals in Krasnokamensk (Russia) and Jinan (China) – assistance from St. Gallen (Switzerland).
- The sub-region R72 will have the capitals in Baguio City (Philippines) and Hangzhou (China) – assistance from Dole (France).
- The sub-region R73 will have the capitals in Manila (Philippines) and Taipei (Taiwan, China) – assistance from Metz (France).

- The sub-region R74 will have the capitals in Kupang (Indonesia) and Shanghai (China) – assistance from Davos (Switzerland).
- The sub-region R75 will have the capitals in Pyongyang (North Korea) and Seoul (South Korea) – assistance from Versailles (France).
- The sub-region R76 will have the capitals in Vladivostok (Russia) and Busan (South Korea) – assistance from Innsbruck (Austria).
- The sub-region R77 will have the capitals in Kyoto (Japan) and Khabarovsk (Russia) – assistance from Germering (Germany).
- The sub-region R78 will have the capitals in Nagoya (Japan) and Komsomolsk-on-Amur (Russia) – assistance from Venice (Italy).
- The sub-region R79 will have the capitals in Sendai (Japan) and Melbourne (Australia) – assistance from St. Moritz (Switzerland).

11 July 2009, from the Northern Avenue, near Seaport Hotel & World Trade Center, looking northeast to tall ships anchored at Boston Fish Pier (the oldest continuously operated fish pier in US).

In Region R8: from Anchorage (Alaska, USA) to Lima (Peru)

- The sub-region R80 will have the capitals in Uelen (Russia) and Anchorage (Alaska, USA), – assistance from Zug (Switzerland).
- The sub-region R81 will have the capitals in Vancouver (Canada) and San Jose (CA, USA) – assistance from Odense (Denmark).
- The sub-region R82 will have the capitals in Vernon (Canada) and Los Angeles (CA, USA) – assistance from Amstetten (Austria).
- The sub-region R83 will have the capitals in Calgary (Canada) and Tijuana (Mexico) – assistance from Chur (Switzerland).
- The sub-region R84 will have the capitals in Hermosillo (Mexico) and Tucson (AR, USA) – assistance from Bergen (Norway).
- The sub-region R85 will have the capitals in Chihuahua (Mexico) and Regina (Canada) – assistance from Gothenburg (Sweden).
- The sub-region R86 will have the capitals in San Luis Potosi City (Mexico) and Winnipeg (Canada) – assistance from Yverdon-les-Bains (Switzerland).
- The sub-region R87 will have the capitals in Tulsa (OK, USA) and Veracruz (Mexico) – assistance from Bregenz (Austria).
- The sub-region R88 will have the capitals in Memphis (TN, USA) and San José (Costa Rica) – assistance from Uppsala (Sweden).
- The sub-region R89 will have the capitals in Lima (Peru) and Boston (MA, USA) – assistance from Tampere (Finland).

Rome: Curia (left), Caesar's Forum (center), Nerva's Forum (down).

In Region R9: from La Paz (Bolivia) to London (United Kingdom)

- The sub-region R90 will have the capitals in La Paz (Bolivia) and Bangor (Maine, USA) – assistance from Aosta (Italy).
- The sub-region R91 will have the capitals in Caracas (Venezuela) and Road Town (British Virgin Islands) – assistance from Obergoms (Switzerland).
- The sub-region R92 will have the capitals in Buenos Aires (Argentina) and Fort-de-France (Martinique) – assistance from Freudenstadt (Germany).
- The sub-region R93 will have the capitals in Asuncion (Paraguay) and Montevideo (Uruguay) – assistance from Winterthur (Switzerland).
- The sub-region R94 will have the capitals in Cayenne (French Guiana), St. John's (Canada) – assistance from Novara (Italy).
- The sub-region R95 will have the capitals in Rio de Janeiro (Brazil) and Dakar (Senegal) – assistance from Toyama (Japan).
- The sub-region R96 will have the capitals in Freetown (Sierra Leone) and Lisbon (Portugal) – assistance from Kawasaki (Japan).
- The sub-region R97 will have the capitals in Bamako (Mali) and Athlone (Ireland) – assistance from Ulm (Germany).
- The sub-region R98 will have the capitals in Yamoussoukro (Cote d'Ivoire) and Madrid (Spain) – assistance from Okayama (Japan).
- The sub-region R99 will have the capitals in Ouagadougou (Burkina Faso) and London (United Kingdom) - assistance from Vaasa (Finland).

1.3. 1000 Districts with 7.7 M each

Each of the 100 sub-regions from 1.2 above will be divided in 10 districts D000, D001,   , D999, each with about 7.7 M people.

Therefore, our Planet Earth will have 10 regions, 100 sub-regions, and 1,000 districts, each of the districts with their current small and big cities.

We'll have 1,000 Level 1 friendly managers for the 1,000 districts, who will supervise and assist the mayors and town managers from their district, for a total of about 7,700,000 people in each district. Each of the 1,000 L1 friendly managers will be located in a central city from their districts – they could be the mayors of those cities, but with new responsibilities for the whole district – one main responsibility will be no bureaucracy.

Italy, Rome (753 BC), Villa Borghese (1630), Lake Garden, from Viale del Lago, Tempio di Esculapio (1786, Temple of Asclepius (god of medicine, healing, rejuvenation and physicians)) on artificial island; on front, in Greek "To Asclepius the savior".

2- Four Levels of World Non-bureaucratic Management

7. 7 B people need four levels (4 levels will have less bureaucracy; however, at the local level could be one or two levels of local managers (mayors, town managers, county managers)) of non-bureaucratic world management:

- Level 1: 1,000 L1 friendly managers for the 1,000 districts, who will supervise and assist the mayors and town managers from their district, for a total of about 7,700,000 people each district.

- Level 2: 100 L2 friendly managers for the 100 sub-regions, who will supervise and assist the 10 L1 managers of the 10 districts of each sub-region, for a total of about 78,000,000 people each sub-region.

- Level 3: 10 L3 friendly managers for the 10 regions, who will supervise and assist the 10 L2 managers of the 10 sub-regions of each region, for a total of about 780,000,000 people each region.

- Level 4: L4 very friendly 10 Advisers of the world, who will supervise and assist the 10 L3 managers of the 10 regions of the Earth, for a total of about 7,700,000,000 people – all the people on Earth.

2.1 10 Advisers for all 7.7 B people on Earth

The top management will be formed of 10 Advisers, elected from the 10 regions, and each of them will be the First Adviser (*First among equals* – from Latin: Primus inter pares) for one month, by rotation. They will move each month from a first capital of a region to the second capital of another region, at random (or based on urgency, if an emergency occurred). After its very good work, the United Nations will change into World Police and Assistance Organization (WPAO), to help local police in case of big natural disasters or big accidents, and will report to the top 10 Advisers.

The L4 very friendly 10 Advisers of the world will be located each in one the ten Regions R0, R1,..., R9. For example, in the beginning, for the first month (then changing every month), the ten Advisers of the world will be located:

- in R0: Barcelona (Spain)
- in R1: Benghazi (Libya)
- in R2: Addis Ababa (Ethiopia)
- in R3: Hyderabad (Pakistan)
- in R4: Bhopal (India)
- in R5: Mandalay (Myanmar)
- in R6: Nanchong (China)
- in R7: Khabarovsk (Russia)
- in R8: Houston (USA)
- in R9: Recife (Brazil)

The First Adviser, on the last day of each month, will present in writing for the world (no more than 5 standard pages) a clear and precise Monthly World Report, with a list of finished and unfinished tasks.

The other 9 Advisers will add their comments to the Monthly World Report (no more than half a page each - total report less than 9.5 pages).

Advisors (and all the others) cannot declare war, reprisals or capture land or water.

Advisors (and all the others) cannot raise and support armies, navy, or any military forces.

All people live in an age of growing frustrations, conflicts, war-preparations, and uncertainties, and it's difficult to enjoy life, but shortly, with major positive changes based on the World Constitution, people will let go of qualms, doubts, and obstructions, and finally will experience profounder joy, smiling serenity, and strong self-confidence

USA, New York: from W 34th St, looking northeast to Seventh Ave (Fashion Ave).

2.2. Advisers will be elected every 20 months

The Advisers will be elected every 20 months for one term only. If an Adviser X was elected for a term T1, then the next term T2 will have another Advisor Y. For the next term T3, X can be elected again, but the next term T4 will have a new Adviser, and so on. An Advisor can be elected, not consecutively, at most 4 times (80 months = 6 years and 8 months).

Advisers should have exceptional results obtained from their work, and based on these results, plus modesty, moderation, good character, friendliness, sharp mind, wisdom, good morals, and intense desire to help people, they will be elected, without any campaigning, publicity, fundraising, donations, debates, propaganda, political parties, advertising, or similar activities.

In order to better know the world government, to help it, and, especially, to improve it, all able people of the world will work as volunteers at least one day per year in each of the seven departments.

After each Monthly World Report, a public opinion survey about the report should be taken, and presented to all Advisors.

3 – Level 4: All 7.7 B people on Earth - World Level Non-Bureaucratic Management

The top 10 L4 friendly Advisers, which were elected from the 10 regions, are the world level managers, responsible for the Earth population of over 7,700,000,000 people, and, as a team, will daily discuss with, and practically assist, the 10 L3 managers of the 10 regions, and will continuously work for improvements at the world level:

- All 10 Advisers must be much closer to the people
- All the budgets based on these taxes must have a 2% surplus.
- With this new structure, we have just one country – Terra, and everybody is a citizen of Terra.
- the top management will be formed of 10 Advisers Level 4, each of them will be the First Adviser for one month, by rotation.
- They will work by consensus only.
- People will always be able to change some Advisors, if they do not perform at the expected level – simply present a petition and count electronically how many people agree. If more than half of the people who voted for a certain Advisor X want to change X, then X will be changed with the number 2 for that district.

3.1. 5 Assistants

- Each Advisor, and each manager at all levels, will have 5 immediate assistants:
1) a mathematician for finance and all other calculations,
2) a medical doctor for keeping everybody healthy, calm, polite, friendly and optimist,
3) a CEO for good management,
4) an engineer for all practical projects, and
5) a teacher for education, training and related areas.

- The top 10 Advisers (and all the other managers) will collaborate via e-mail, telephone, videoconferences, mail, or face to face, when needed, to produce practical results for all people, very fast.

- Advisors with disorderly behavior will be medically treated, and, when necessary, will be changed with their number 2.

- All the activities of all Advisors will be recorded in computers and videos, and on paper, such that the people who are interested, to be able to see what they are doing.

- Because the objective is not to have any conflicts on Earth, the secrecy will slowly disappear.

- Advisors and managers at all levels will work 40 hours/week, with 4 weeks vacation, but many services (medical, police (firemen should be part of the police), volunteers) should be non-stop.

- At least 7 of the top 10 Advisers should be present every working day.

– The five assistants play a key role, because they are highly qualified professionals, who actually will carry on the practical management of the world.

- The five assistants' integrity, professionalism and friendliness will significantly improve the quality of the world and local governments.

- The five assistants are really the experts. They will assist the Advisors and all levels of management, in order to have an efficient, correct and professional working of the world government at all levels.

Rome: Via di San Gregorio and the Arch of Constantine (315 AD, left), and the Amphitheatrum Flavium (Colosseum, 80 AD, right).

3.2. Advisors' compensation

- Top ten Advisors' compensation should be the world annual average salary. They all should work to increase the world average salary, in order to get themselves an increase.

- All the other world government employees will have a compensation close the average compensation of the people in the area where they are located.

France, Paris: Galeries Lafayette (1895) a classy store on Blvd Haussmann (right), near Rue La Fayette (center-left).

4 – Non-bureaucratic World Government

- All the employees in the World Government are temporary, and must reapply for their positions every year.

- No need for unions.

- The World Government will be limited to:
1) the Office of the Honorific Observer (less than 10 employees),
2) the Office of the 10 Advisors (less than 100 employees), and
3) 7 small departments.

USA, New York: on 5th Ave, the southeast façade of the New York Public Library (1902).

4.1. Honorific World Observer

An Honorific World Observer will be quietly elected by direct vote – starting, let's say September 1st, 2022 - for only one 3 years term, with the request to observe that the top 10 Advisers efficiently perform their duties, and keep their words – if they don't, they must be changed.

For managers and for everybody else, keeping their word is a serious and strict requirement.

The Office of the Honorific World Observer will have less than 10 employees.

Switzerland: from Genève to Thoiry (France), on Route de Meyrin, 2 km west from Geneva Cointrin Airport, there is this renovation of the external structural Elements of the Globe of Science and Innovation.

4.2. Non-bureaucratic Rules proposed by Advisers

- All rules proposed by Advisers must be approved by their 5 assistants (doctors, mathematicians, CEOs, engineers and teachers), and for any new rule over 2,000 basic rules (each rule on at most half a page, total 1,000 pages), at least on old rule must be eliminated.

- All the government work, which can be done be private companies, will be contracted with the best and reasonably priced private companies.

- All Advisors and managers are free to speak about their administrative work, with modesty

- Advisors (and all the other managers) cannot declare war, reprisals or capture land or water.

- Advisors (and all the other managers) cannot raise and support armies, navy, or any military forces.

- The Advisors will be located in the current government buildings, and the excess government buildings and properties will be sold, in order to increase the budget, and to reduce the expenses.

- Not many rules will be necessary, because the people will be more civilized and friendly, and the common sense (in Latin: ad iudicium) will be the main rule.

- All the activity of the Advisors, and others from the small World Government, will be available to the people on a website.

4.3. No abuses

- Special attention will be given by Advisors to avoid abuses and wrong interpretations of the rules. All assistants (doctors, mathematicians, CEOs, engineers and teachers) will closely monitor all activities, to avoid abuses and wrong interpretations of the rules.

- The speech should be free, and is expected not to call for war, violence, or similar destructive activities. People want peace, freedom, health, friendship and prosperity.

- The press should be free, and is expected not to call for war, violence, or similar destructive activities. People want peace, freedom, health, friendship and prosperity.

- People can assemble peacefully only, with police for help, and is expected not to call for war, violence, or similar destructive activities. People want peace, freedom, health, friendship and prosperity.

- People of course can petition the small Word Government, and can change it anytime, if it does not perform as expected.

- Arms will not exist anymore, and only the police will have some small arms. Those who want arms for hunting or sport, will rent them from police stations, with proper documents, rules and payments.

4.4. Volunteers especially for bureaucracy elimination

In order to better know the world government, to help it, and, especially, to improve it, all able people of the world will work as volunteers at least one day per year in each of the seven departments, especially for bureaucracy elimination.

People want peace, freedom, health, friendship and prosperity, therefore conflicts should be quickly resolved, and then the corrective medical treatment will include the transformation of hostility and aggressiveness into harmony and friendship.

USA, Washington (1790), National Gallery of Art (1937, National Mall).

4 eople

In order to prevent bad things, the police, doctors and other assistants will be in permanent non-bureaucratic contact with all the people, by visiting them, phone calls, e-mails, videos, and mail, to keep everybody calm and friendly.

Japan, Osaka, ladies in kimono (means thing to wear, now it is very formal and polite clothing, generally worn with traditional footwear (zori or geta) and with split-toe socks (tabi)).

4.6. Common language and alphabet

For obvious reasons, including the elimination of bureaucracy, it is normal to have a common language and alphabet on Earth. Because English is a de facto common language now, it will be taken as the basis of the world language, let's call it Mundo, which will be taught in all schools and used in the world government. All the other languages will continue as secondary languages.

The same is true for the Latin alphabet, which will be used everywhere, with other alphabets as secondary.

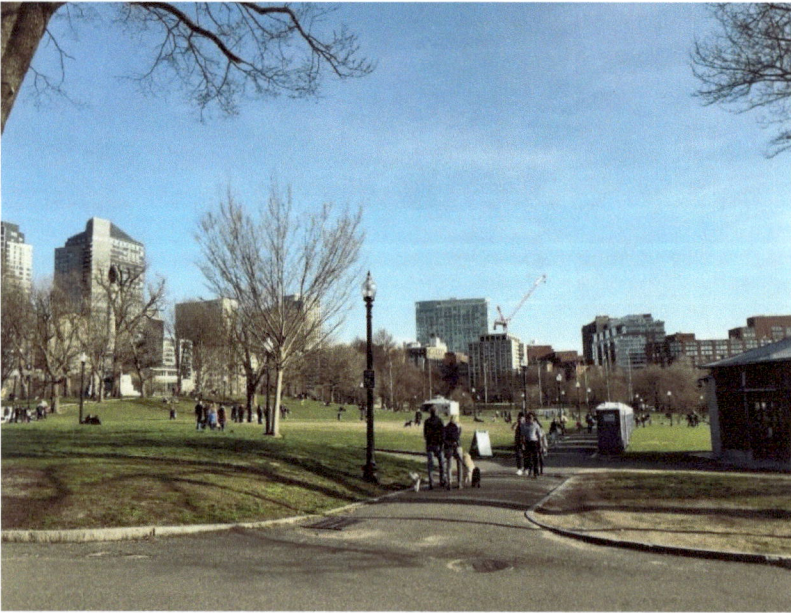

USA, Boston, 16 April 2016, from the north side of the Boston Common, looking southeast to buildings on Boylston St (right) and Tremont St (left).

4.7. Non-bureaucratic work for everybody

Non-bureaucratic work for everybody: when somebody X is unemployed, X can ask for a temporary world minimum wage ($2/hour) job (assisting other people, for example), until X finds a better job.

Important to know - who wants to work for the world government must have good manners and good non-bureaucratic skills.

Rome: Trajan's column (113, center-left), la Chiesa Santissimo Nome di Maria al Foro Traiano. The columns were part of Basilica Ulpia.

4.8. Ten world holidays

Ten world holidays: the normal 4 Earth events (2 solstices (21 or 22 June, 21 or 22 December), and 2 equinoxes (21 or 22 March, 21 or 22 September), Mother's Day on 1st May, Father's Day on 6 August, Children's Day on 6 November, Grandparents' Day on 6 February, and 2 optional days (like Thanksgiving or a Religious Day (Christmas), and New Year).

UK, Cambridge: from Trinity Ln, looking west to the entrance of Trinity Hall (1350, a constituent college (the 5th oldest) of the University of Cambridge).

USA, Boston: a beautiful tall ship on the north-west side of the Boston Fish Pier. Bostonians welcome tall ships and their crews and cadets, from all over the world, to their harbor, on a continuous basis

5 – Non-bureaucratic Tax Department

Collects taxes of 15% of the income of people and revenue of companies.

The Manager of the Tax Department is appointed for a three-year term by the World 10 Advisers.

The number of employees must be under 50,000, with excellent computers, and advanced software.

It will have a small police group for protection of the facilities.

Italy, Rome (753 BC), Arcus Constantini (315, Constantine I (born 272, emperor 306-337)) and Amphitheatrum Flavium (right 80, started by Flavius Vespasian (born 9 AD, emperor 69-79) in 70 and completed by his son Titus Flavius Vespasianus (born 39, emperor 79-81) in 80, wrongly called Colosseum).

5.1. Current buildings and equipment

All current buildings and equipment can be used, with improvements and modifications.

It will have a small medical group to assist the employees, the taxpayers who need stress relief, and to eliminate bureaucracy and conflicts.

UK: typical houses on the road from Crewkerne to East Lambrook (8 km north, with the Anglican Church of St James from around 1150).

5.2. Taxpayer assistance group

It will have a taxpayer assistance group, for elderly, sick, and taxpayers with other severe issues.

Completely eliminate corruption, organized crime, drug trafficking and bureaucracy.

In order to better know the world government, to help it, and, especially, to improve it (especially by eliminating bureaucracy), all able people of the world will work as volunteers at least one day per year in the local facility of this tax department, which will have a special office for managing this volunteer work.

Canada, Niagara Falls: the American Falls (21-30 m drop, 290 m wide, left), and the Horseshoe Falls (in Canada, 53 m drop, 790 m wide, right), with a boat with tourists (left) and a rainbow.

6 – Non-bureaucratic Treasury

It will control all the financial issues, including:
- antitrust
- fiscal service
- financial cooperation
- assist all people to have savings accounts for old age (the old age will be starting around 70), and 10% of their income should automatically go to their savings accounts. For those unable to work, their doctors and mathematicians will decide case by case.
- no bureaucracy
- The World Central Bank will include all current central banks – starting, for example, on May 1st, 2023.
- The Special Credit Card (SCC) will be issued by the World Central Bank.

From the northwest corner of the Tower of London (left), looking southwest to the Shard. From around 1350 for 300 years the coronation procession started here at the Tower, ending at Westminster Abbey (4 km west (right

6.1. Currency control

- Advisors will create a new world currency, named, let's say "coin", and all the other currencies will be exchanged for coins.

The World Central Bank will implement the details.

Italy, Rome, Forum Caesaris (46 BC, by Julius Caesar (100 – 44 BC), with Temple of Venus Genetrix (center)), Via dei Fori Imperiali (left), Chiesa dei Santi Luca e Martina (right, 625, 1669).

6.2. Banks

- financing bank
- world reserve system
- world budget using only revenue, no borrowing, and spending only on strict necessary needs – always with 2% surplus returned to taxpayers

USA, Boston, 3 Dec 2009, from Avenue Louis Pasteur (1822-1895, French microbiologist), Boston Public Latin School (1635, Schola Latina Bostoniensis, the oldest and the first public exam school in the U.S.).

6.3. Accounting standards

- register of all government papers and activities
- archives and records

Standards will be necessary in many areas, in order for all people to be able to have access to all products

UK, London, at the east end of Westminster Bridge (1862, 250 m, width 26 m, 7 spans, right) over Thames (flowing left to right), Palace of Westminster (1016, 1870, 300 m river front façade, 1,100 rooms, center left, with Victoria Tower (1858, 98 m, left), and Central Tower (91 m)), Big Ben (Elizabeth Tower, 1855, 96 m, center right).

6.4. Savings account for retirement

- Everybody will have a savings account for retirement (the retirement will be starting around 70), and 10% of their income will automatically go to their savings accounts. For those unable to work, their doctors and mathematicians will decide case by case. All families will assist their parents, grandparents, and great-grandparents.
- All spending proposals from Advisers must be approved by their 5 assistants (doctors, mathematicians, CEOs, engineers and teachers), and must have an already existing funding in the budget.

Paris: L'Église de la Madeleine (Magdalenae, or L'Église Sainte-Marie-Madeleine, or La Madeleine, 1842), a Roman Catholic Church in the 8th arrondissement of Paris, designed by Napoleon in 1806.

6.5. Non-bureaucratic Mortgages

- housing finance
- housing for all people
- no homelessness
- All people in the world will remain in their places, and the improvements will come to them. Those who want to move to other places, will need first a special invitation from at least 10 people (not family related) where they want to move.
- credit when strict necessary
- consumer financial protection
- pensions
- privacy
- current social security until replaced by personal savings
- investor advises
- securities
- insurance: bank deposit, flood, auto, house, life, etc.

6.6. Personnel management

- ethics,
- discipline
- bureaucracy is an issue that must be eliminated
- receiving comments from people
- completely eliminate corruption, organized crime and drug trafficking
- constant attention will be focused on avoiding duplication at all levels of the world government – there must be continuous collaboration between all levels, to prevent duplication and to eliminate it, if it was found.

Rome: John Cabot University (1972), American University in Rome

6.7. Non-bureaucratic general services for the world government

- procurement
- vendor
- contractors, etc.
- merit systems
- inspectors on integrity and efficiency
- peace volunteers
- Bankruptcies, in general, will be discouraged, and when strict necessary, will be analyzed and solved, case by case, by the doctors, mathematicians and CEOs who worked with the people who asked the bankruptcy.
- All the rules can be changed or eliminated when a majority of the people or their Advisors agree, but some fundamental peace, freedom and order rules will remain.

- In order to better know the world government, to help it, and, especially, to improve it, all able people of the world will work as volunteers at least one day/year in the local facility of this Treasury department, which will have a special office for managing this volunteer work.

7 – Non-bureaucratic People Assistance Department

It will assist people in general, including:
- helping people to be friendly and happy
- living in harmony
- parent assistance

UK, London, the upper part of the western façade and entrance of Westminster Abbey (960, 1517, Anglican abbey with daily services, and all coronations since 1066, tower height 69 m).

7.1. Dispute resolution

- appeals
- reporting
- census

In very simple disputes or culpa levis (ordinary negligence, like late payments, etc.), one single assistant will decide within minutes, and all people will go back to work

The medical personnel and others will work diligently to make sure that disputes are resolved, and then a friendship is developed. Only in this way the situation will become stable.

Venice: Monumento a Vittorio Emanuele II, with Londra Palace (back), on Riva degli Schiavoni.

7.2. Non-bureaucratic election assistance

- people will be elected from the neighborhood up, based on merit appreciated by the people, not on political parties, not on propaganda, etc.
- No fundraising, no donations asked by e-mails, phone calls, or mail, no begging of any type.
- Leadership is important for getting good results; therefore, much attention should be paid when electing leaders.
- All managers must have strong desire to succeed in the tasks given to them by the people.
- Advisers should have exceptional results obtained from their work, and based on these results, plus modesty, moderation, good character, friendliness, sharp mind, wisdom, good morals, and intense desire to help people, they will be elected, without any campaigning, publicity, fundraising, donations, debates, propaganda, political parties, advertising, or similar activities.
- It is highly recommended the use of advanced digital technology, which opens up entirely new opportunities for developing direct democracy, and public control institutions, improving the transparency of the election procedure, and taking into account the interests and opinions of each voter. Cybersecurity will not be a problem, because of the strict discipline on the users of computers and communications.
- Voters are people over the age of 21, who are not in a special medical institution for bad behavior or for mental health.
- voting administration

7.3. Special credit cards

- special credit cards for all people for identification, medical assistance, vaccination, purchases, etc.

The Special Credit Card (SCC) will be issued by the World Central Bank.

Italy, Gate 2 to the ruins of Pompeii (650 BC, in 79 covered by ash), with a panel entitled CARPE DIEM (enjoy the day), a Latin aphorism from a poem in the Odes (book 1, number 11) in 23 BC by the Roman poet Horace (Quintus Horatius Flaccus, born December 8, 65 BC in Venusia, Roman Republic, died November 27, 8 BC, in Rome, the capital of the Roman Empire). Important lyric poetry volumes are Odes, Satires and Ars Poetica.

7.4. People protection against abuses

- people protection against abuses from anybody
- mediation
- conciliation
- people movement assistance
- completely eliminate corruption, organized crime, drug trafficking, and bureaucracy

USA, New York: Times Square: 7th Ave (right straight), Broadway (center straight), W 43rd St (left and right), Marriott Marquis (right), Bertelsmann Building (left), Conde Nast Building (next), looking south.

7.5. Food safety

- inspection
- nutrition
- agriculture
- pesticide

USA, Newport, the western façade of Marble House, 1888-1892, 50 rooms, 14,000 m^3 of marble, 1.6 ha, William Kissam Vanderbilt (1849-1920, younger brother of Cornelius), and his wife Alva (1853-1933).

7.6. Trash & recycling

- trash & recycling
- use of private companies with advanced technology
- prevention of accidents, etc.
- cooperation

Italy, Roma, Theatrum Marcelli (the Theatre of Marcellus (Marcus Claudius Marcellus, 42 BC – 23 BC, nephew of the emperor Augustus, who named this theatre after him in 11 BC)), near the Tiber river.

7.7. Non-bureaucratic Commerce

- The commerce between the people on the Earth will be free of taxes, tariffs, duties, etc. - plenty of opportunities for everybody

Romania, Sibiu (25 km south of Şeica Mare, and 90 km southwest of Târgu Mureş), 11 Oct 2008, in the Small Square, looking northwest to the Liars Bridge (1859, the first footbridge in Romania to have been cast in iron, its name comes from stories and tall talk of the nearby hagglers selling fish, center), and a bride being photographed (down).

7.8. Jobs

- jobs assistance
- retirement assistance

There will always be plenty of jobs at world minimum wage (assisting other people, for example), and the standard situation will be this: more jobs than available people, so people will choose the jobs they like the most.

Venezia: Palazzo Flangini (right) and other palazzini on the north bank of Canal Grande, 220 m east of Ponte degli Scalzi.

7.9. Non-bureaucratic postal service

- postal service inspection
- World Post Offices will include the current ones, which will be interconnected, improved and modernized.
- parks

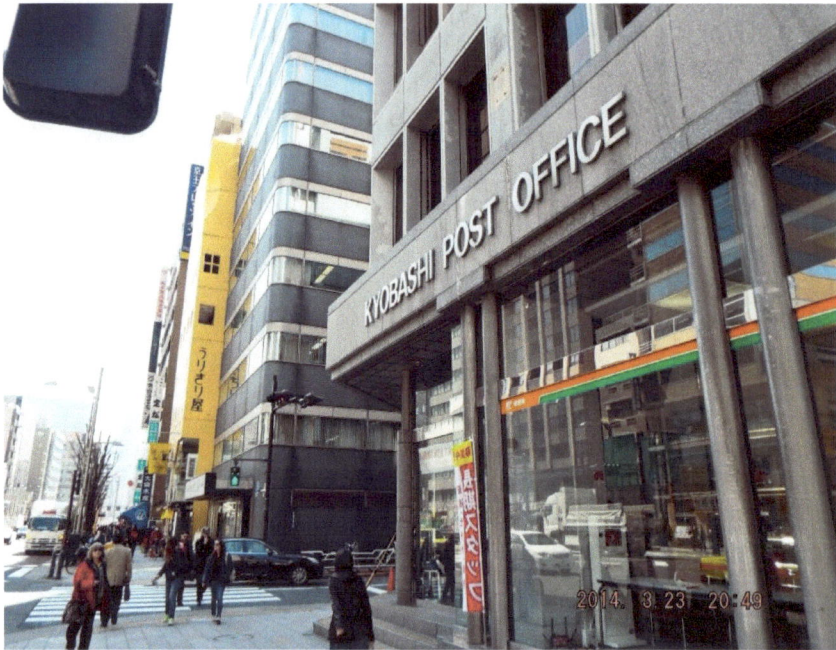

Japan, Tokyo, Kyobashi Post Office on Harumi Dori, near Tsukiji Bus Station, Tully's Coffee and Tokyo Metro Hibiya Line.

7.10. Non-bureaucratic rural and urban planning and development

- rural and urban business, planning and development,
- improving rural broadband
- assistance to refugees from disasters

Italia, Venezia, Ponte di Rialto (1588 – 1591) with Fermata Rialto (right), seen from south.

7.11. Non-bureaucratic labor safety and harmonious relations

- labor safety
- harmonious relations
- employees and employers harmony

UK, London, from the northwest corner of Trafalgar Square (1840), looking northeast to The National Gallery (1824, over 2,300 paintings, left), St. Martin in the Fields Church (1724, right, with music recitals).

7.12. Non-bureaucratic land and water management

- land management
- water
- water treatment
- plumbing
- sewer
- zoning

Switzerland, Lausanne (Roman 150, 147,000, 41 km^2, 500 m elevation, 62 km northeast of Geneva, the home of the International Olympic Committee), marina on Lac Léman, southwest of Place de la Navigation (right).

7.13. Non-bureaucratic fisheries management and sustainability

- fisheries management and sustainability
- animal and insect control
- forest
- cemetery administration

UK, London, from a boat on Thames (flowing left to right), looking southwest to the Westminster Bridge (1862, 250 m), the east (left) and north sides of Palace of Westminster (1016, 1870), Big Ben (1855, 96 m, right).

7.14. Non-bureaucratic Volunteers Management

- volunteers to help people
- In order to better know the world government, to help it, and, especially, to improve it, all able people of the world will work as volunteers at least one day/year in the local facility of this department, which will have a special office for managing this volunteer work.
- religious activity
- The religion should be free, and is expected not to interfere with activities of the Advisors, and actually should help people.
- gaming under strict supervision

Forum Nervae (97, down), Forum Augusti (2 BC, with Temple of Mars Ultor, built with white marble of Carrara, center-right-up).

7.15. Fitness, sport, tourism

- fitness
- sport
- tourism
- public events
- beautification
- Nobility (King, Prince, etc.) could continue to exist in some places, but they should not interfere with activities of the Advisors, and actually should help them.

9 April 2021. People express deepest condolences to Queen Elizabeth II, and to all the members of the royal family, on the passing of Queen Elizabeth II's husband Prince Philip, Duke of Edinburgh (10 June 1921, Mon Repos, Corfu, Greece – 9 April 2021, Windsor Castle, Windsor, United Kingdom, age 99 years 9 months and 30 days, married to Queen Elizabeth II for 74 years (from 1947)). People wish Queen Elizabeth II strength and resilience in the face of this severe loss.

Notes: Just 4.5 months after the birth of Prince Philip of Greece, his cousin Prince Mihai of Romania was born in Peles Castle, Romania, on 25 October 1921. There are splendid photos of Philip and Mihai, taken in 1927, when they were around 6 years old, on horses near Constanta, Romania, playing in a garden near Sibiu, Romania, and on a balcony of a house in Bucharest, Romania. Then, around 1939, around 18 years old, on a well in a nice yard, near the Peles Castle, Romania. Mihai I, former King of Romania, passed on 5 December 2017, age 96 years and 11 days, in Aubonne, Switzerland, then buried in Curtea de Arges, Romania.

France, Paris: Place de la Concorde: the north side of the Egyptian obelisk (circa 1250 BC), with hieroglyphics about the pharaoh Ramses the Great (1303 BC – 1213 BC (90 years), reign 1279 BC – 1213 BC (66 years)). The obelisk is from Luxor, rises 23 m, weights 250 t and it was placed here by the King Louis Philippe I (1773 – 1850, reign 1830 – 1848) in 1836, On the pedestal are drawn diagrams showing the techniques used for transportation. The original cap was stolen in Luxor around 550 BC, and the French Government added a gold-leafed pyramid cap in 1998.

8 - Medical Department

It will manage all medical and healthcare related areas, including human services, and conflict resolution.

- For simple administrative disagreements, an Administrator from another region will serve as mediator, together with a medical doctor, a mathematician, a CEO (and other specialists as needed), for solving the disagreements in a matter of minutes or hours (maximum 10 hours).

The lasting dividends of good health are really significant.

Rome: Accademia Nazionale dei Lincei (1603, the oldest worldwide) has its library in Palazzo Corsini (1740), Via della Lungara 10, Roma.

8.1. Families

- families
- children
- child support
- elderly

We always start with the big family of over 7.7 billions of people living on Earth.

Like in any big family, there will be differences in organization and management, based on their abilities and objectives, but all must be peaceful and harmonious.

All people must be able to communicate easily with each other.

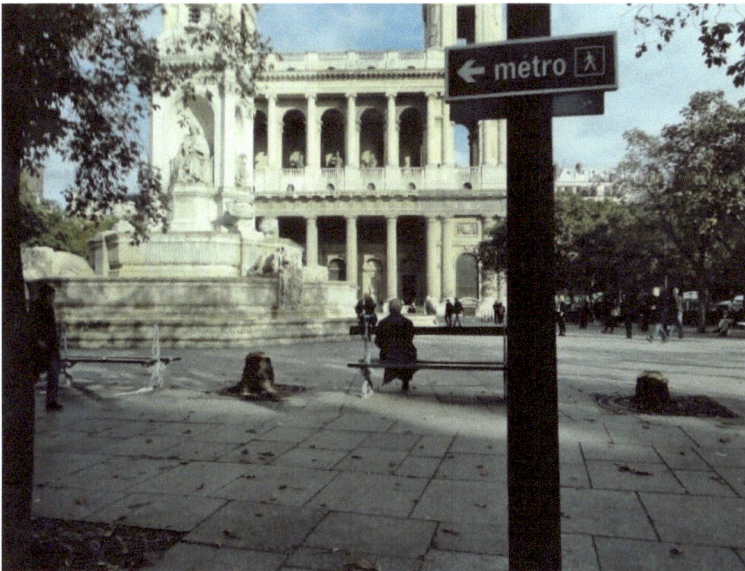

Paris: Place Saint-Sulpice, east from Rue Bonaparte, with Fontaine Saint-Sulpice and l'Église Saint-Sulpice (1646-1780, 113x58x34 m, second largest after Notre-Dame), north-west of Jardin du Luxembourg.

8.2. Non-bureaucratic medicine approval

- medicine approval
- medical cooperation
- veterans
- community living
- toxic substances

There will be government pharmaceutical institutions and private pharmaceutical companies, offering reasonable priced medicines, without advertising to the general public

Switzerland, Geneva (121 BC under Romans), Avenue de la Paix 19, International Committee of the Red Cross, founded by Jean Henri Dunant (1828-1910) on Feb. 9, 1863, three Nobel Peace Prizes.

8.3. Disease control and prevention

- disease control and prevention
- infection prevention
- animal control
- seafood and plant health inspection

France, Lyon (43 BC), part of eastern façade of the Hôtel de Ville (1645 – 1651, 1674) de Lyon, in Place de la Comédie, across Opéra.

8.4. Home visits

- home visits
- treatment at home, etc.
- Medical doctors and assistants will make regular home visits to all people, to keep them healthy, and to prevent illnesses.

Italy, Venezia, Palazzi Erizzo (left), Soranzo (center) and Emo (right), on the north bank, 400 m east of Ponte degli Scalzi.

8.5. Medical research

- medical research: cancer, heart, lung, blood, arthritis, surgical robotics, connected computers for healthcare, etc.
- prevention of sickness
- disability assistance
- healthy homes, streets, stores, working places, etc.
- healthy aging
- air quality
- special medical institutions for substance abuse and mental health, including correction of aggressive sick people.
- All misunderstandings, disagreements or conflicts of any nature will be treated by medical personnel (with police help when strict necessary), until all is back to normal. No prisons are necessary, only specialized medical institutions (in simple cases, the places where the treated people live can be used, with the necessary limitations and surveillance).

Constanța, Romania, Piazza Ovidiu: Statue of Publius Ovidius Naso (20 March 43 BC, in Sulmona – 17, in Tomis, Moesia (now Constanța, Romania), aged 60

8.6. Volunteers for healthcare

- volunteers to help sick people
- to give health information.
- Medical volunteers' sympathy and goodness are noble traditions, as well as their compassion, which help to resolve serious healthcare tasks, cooperating with medical institutions, doing the important job of educating and promoting the values of a healthy lifestyle, and encouraging voluntary work.
- In order to better know the world government, to help it, and, especially, to improve it, all able people of the world will work as volunteers at least one day/year in the local facility of this department, which will have a special office for managing this volunteer work.

UK, Cambridge, from the south gate of Trinity College (1546) Great Court (which is the main court), looking north to the northern part of the Great Court (the largest enclosed court in Europe).

8.7. Non-bureaucratic Medical insurance

– All people will have government medical insurance, and they can also have private medical insurance.

– There will be doctors working for the government 100%, or only part-time, or having only private practice, all with reasonable salaries and fees.

Italy, the entrance to the modern city of Pompei, located southeast of the ruins of the ancient Pompeii (650 BC, in 79 covered by ash).

8.8. Non-bureaucratic Pharmaceutical institutions

– There will be government pharmaceutical institutions and private pharmaceutical companies, offering reasonable priced medicines, without advertising to the general public.

- COVID-19 had a great impact on all pharmaceutical companies – much improvement is necessary – too much bureaucracy, too little qualified medical personnel.

UK, Cambridge, inside the Old Court of Clare College (1326, 1638-1715), looking west to the western part of the Old Court.

9 - Police

Police will provide assistance in:
- accidents
- disasters

Police will always assist people in need.

Conflicts will be promptly resolved by the medical personnel, police, and other assistants.

Police will be people's friends everywhere.

USA, Cambridge, 23 September 2009, on the campus of Harvard University (1636) in Cambridge, The Harry Elkins Widener (1885-1912 (died on Titanic)) Memorial Library (1915, Beaux-Arts architecture, 3.5 M of books).

9.1. All arms elimination

- nuclear, chemical and biological arms, firearms and explosives complete elimination,
- world complete security
- world cooperation

Arms will not exist anymore, and only the police will have some small arms.

Italy, Rome (753 BC), Piazza del Campidoglio (1546 by Michelangelo, paving completed in 1940, on Collis Capitolinus, the oldest part of Rome, with Temple of Jupiter (509 BC)), a replica of the equestrian bronze statue (175, the oldest, moved here in 1538) of Marcus Aurelius (born 121, Emperor 161-180), Palazzo Senatorio (right, 1350, bell-tower 1582, atop Tabularium, now the city hall), Palazzo Nuovo (left, 1603-1654, opened 1734).

9.2. Non-bureaucratic conflict resolution

- conflict reduction and resolution
- investigations
- emergency assistance
- training

For example, a better way to overcome the Nagorno-Karabakh conflict is this: take away all the arms from the region, bring in plenty of medical personnel, teachers, businessmen and neutral police, have them discuss with the local people what they really want, then bring in significant economic, medical, educational and police assistance, until the local people can begin to work and support themselves, living in peace, no arms, freedom, harmony and prosperity for all – thus the problem will be solved in several months.

UK, London: from a bus near an Omega shop on Oxford Street at North Audley Street (to the right), building with columns (left), balloons (up).

9.3. Non-bureaucratic delinquency prevention, especially juvenile

- delinquency prevention in general, and especially juvenile
- protection of Advisors, important government buildings, etc.
- extended surveillance and reconnaissance to prevent bad events
- fire protection

Italy, Rome (753 BC), on Via dei Fori Imperiali (for pedestrians only on holidays), Amphitheatrum Flavium (80, called Colosseum, back), Basilica of Maxentius and Constantine (312, right).

9.4. Volunteers for police

- volunteers to help police
- In order to better know the world government, to help it, and, especially, to improve it, all able people of the world will work as volunteers at least one day/year in the local facility of this department, which will have a special office for managing this volunteer work.

Volunteers, as always, will be very important to create and maintain a civilized society.

USA, Boston: a view of the north-east part of Boston, from Cambridge, over Charles River Basin. Federal Reserve Bank Building (187 m, left), and other tall buildings in the financial district.

9.5. Protect the public

- police will be present at public meetings, services, shows, etc., in order to protect the public
- public order
- ensuring traffic safety
- completely eliminate corruption, organized crime and drug trafficking
- movement of people based on rules
- assist and protect those who have encountered violence

UK, Cambridge: from the center of Trinity College (1546) Great Court, looking northeast to the western façade of the Main Gate (center left), and other buildings on the eastern side (right) of the Great Court, and part of the southern façade of the Trinity College Chapel (left).

9.6. Mobile and special operations

- World Police and specialists from the former United Nations and Interpol will be ready and very mobile for urgent and special operations, when they are needed.

- Mobility is an essential factor in an advanced society.

Italy, Rome (753 BC), Forum Romanum, the northwest side of Arcus Septimii Severi (left, 203, Septimius Severus (145 – 211)), the northeast side of Templum Saturni (center, 497 BC, 42 BC, 380), Tabularium (right up, 78 BC by Lucius Cornelius Sulla).

9.7. Qualified personnel

- The Police Department must have qualified personnel, who can speak and write correctly and politely.
- Police will have a small unit of medical personnel, teachers, and other specialists, to assist them when needed.

Japan, Kawaguchi, 17 km north-est of Mount Fuji (3776 m); a big Bonsai tree on the right and three smaller ones on the left.

9.8. Small arms

- Police will be the only department which will have some small arms, in order to stop some very bad people (who are very sick).
- A small manufacturing and maintaining arms unit will be part of the Police Department, under strict control.

Palazzo Giustinian (left), Piazza San Marco (center), Palazzo Ducale (center-right), seen from the east end of Canal Grande.

9.9. Prevention first

- Police will work with medical personnel, mathematicians, CEOs, engineers, teachers and others, to make sure that all the people on the Planet are in good mental health, in order to prevent bad situations. This is also a major responsibility of all Advisors.
- Prevention of bad events is the main objective for everybody. If a bad event occurs, the police and their assistants will eliminate the consequences, reestablish the normal situation, and determine why the bad event occurred, in order to improve their activity and prevent such bad events in the future.

- The Advisors will allocate the necessary budget for Police, and Police will assist people in need.

UK, Cambridge: from the south of Trinity College (1546) Great Court, looking north to the northern part of the Great Court, and the upper part of St. John's College (1511) Chapel (center right up).

9.10. Non-bureaucratic, civilized, free and peaceful world

- The police powers will be limited, and they will know and be friend with all the people in their jurisdiction – this is the key element of a civilized, free and peaceful world. If they notice a person with bad intentions, they immediately retain that person and call for a medical assistant (and other assistants, if necessary), to analyze and solve the issue.

Police will play an important role in eliminating the bureaucracy.

Chiesa degli Scalzi (the church of Santa Maria di Nazareth) was built by Baltassarre Longhena in 1654, and the façade made by Giuseppe Sardi is the only one in Venice built with Carrara marble.

10 - Non-bureaucratic Education Department

It will assist education at all levels. Please see also my book listed at number 90 in Bibliography: Our Future Depends on Good World Educations – Moving from frail education to solid education.

- Mundo language and alphabet
- cooperation in education

UK, London, on Spring Gardens, Nr. 66, near the Admiralty Arch (1912), south of Trafalgar Square

10.1. World Library

- libraries, museums, information centers: A World Library will include the Library of Congress and all the other great libraries – they will remain where they are now, but will be digitally interconnected, and accessible from any place in the world.

The World Library will be a good example of a non-bureaucratic institution.

Italy, Rome, on Via delle Quattro Fontane, Palazzo Barberini, 1627-1633, with the Galleria Nazionale d'Arte Antica. Maffeo Barberini (1568-1644) became Pope Urban VIII (1623-1644).

10.2. Adult education

- adult education: technical, career
- training for employment
- management training
- post high school education

Because of the rapid increase in technology, medicine, science and related areas, continuous education will be a necessity for all.

France, Paris, the north-west part of L'Institut de France (1795, moved in 1805 by Napoléon in this baroque building from 1684) is a revered French cultural society with five académies, the most famous being Académie Français (1635) and. Académie des sciences (1666).

10.3. Special education

- special education
- rehabilitative services

People with medical conditions will receive all the necessary education, without bureaucratic formalities.

Italy, 6 April 1978, Pisa, Palazzo della Carovana (1562-1564) now for Scuola Normale Superiore (1810, by Napoleon Bonaparte (1769-1821), 460 students, 6% admission rate, best in Italy

10.4. Universities

- state Universities will receive some assistance
- all Universities will cooperate for peace, freedom, good health, harmony and prosperity in the world.

France, Université Paris 1 Panthéon-Sorbonne (1971, after the division of the University of Paris (Sorbonne, 1150)), on Rue Saint-Jacques (left) and Rue Soufflot (right, to Panthéon (1758 – 1790)).

10.5. Fine arts, music

- fine arts
- music
- crafts
- humanities

All these are strict necessary for a good quality of life for all.

Italy, Venezia, Palazzo Fontana, with Rio di San Felice (left), on the north bank of the Canal Grande, 530 m east of Ponte degli Scalzi.

10.6. Global media ethics and correctness

- global media ethics, correctness, working for peace, freedom, friendship
- completely eliminate corruption, organized crime, drug trafficking and bureaucracy

Serious efforts will be required in all these areas.

France, Paris, The main entrance on the east façade of the Grand Palais des Champs-Élysées (1900), on Avenue Winston Churchill.

10.7. Non-bureaucratic historic peace preservation

- historic peace preservation and education
- scholarships

The history of peace on Earth is important for all people.

USA, Washington, DC (1790): the entrance to the Smithsonian Institution Building (1849-1855), on Jefferson Drive SW.

10.8. World constitution and peace education

- peace education
- world constitution education

Emphasis on education for peace is of first importance.

France, Paris, the monument "Flamme de la Liberté" (1987, 3.5 m in height, a full-sized, gold-leaf-covered replica of the new flame at the upper end of the torch carried in the hand of the Statue of Liberty, New York), in Place de l'Alma, near the Pont de l'Alma, Paris.

10.9. Volunteers for good education

- In order to better know the world government, to help it, and, especially, to improve it, all able people of the world will work as volunteers at least one day per year in the local facility of this department, which will have a special office for managing this volunteer work.

Italia, Venezia, Palazzo Sagredo (right), on the north bank of the Canal Grande, 580 m east of Ponte degli Scalzi.

11 - Science & Technology Department

It will help in the areas of:
- mathematics
- statistics
- science
- technology

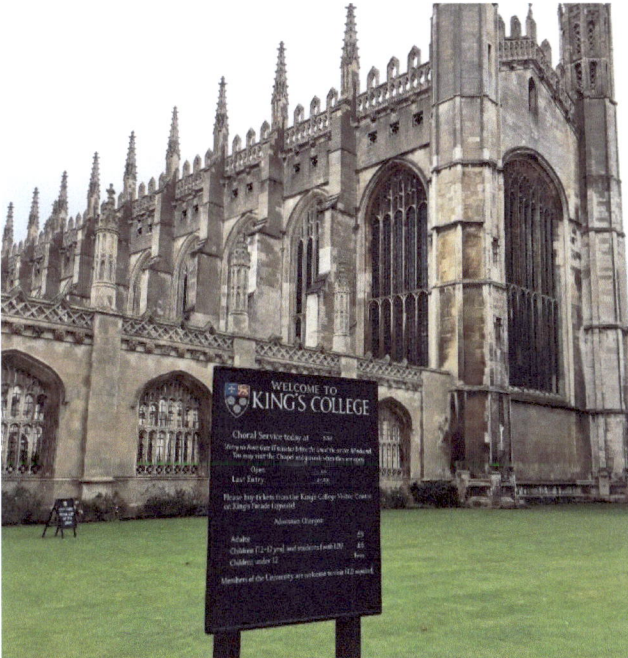

UK, Cambridge, from the entrance to King's College (1441), looking northwest to the Chapel (the south façade (center left), and the east façade (right)).

11.1. Cyberspace complete security

- cyberspace complete security will be achieved and strictly maintained
- information systems
- computer services
- Internet
- scientific cooperation

Because the world digital environment is being used by international terrorists and organized crime, the International Information Security will be based on this cybersecurity for all: all computers will have a place for the user's card – the user's card will have the information about the user, will be registered (for a small fee) with the local cyber-police (which will be connected to the world cyber-police), and the user's card will appear on all the computers contacted by that user, and on user's e-mails. If something unfriendly comes from a computer, it's user card number will be given to the cyber-police, who will immediately contact the user for clarifications and – when necessary – for arrest. Shortly after the implementation of this simple and very efficient cybersecurity method, all computers and information systems will be very safe and friendly, how it was supposed to be from the beginning.

11.2. Energy

- energy industry
- private energy development
- peaceful nuclear energy will be used at the world level

UK, Cambridge: on Trinity Lane, looking east to the southern gate (center) and building of Trinity College (1546, left), and the northwestern building of Gonville and Caius College (1348, 1557, right).

11.3. Non-bureaucratic economic development

- economic development at the world level
- industrial development
- printing
- completely eliminate corruption, organized crime and drug trafficking

USA, Boston: a view of the north part of Boston, from Cambridge, over Charles River Basin. The tall building is Hancock Place (241 m) in Copley Square. To the right is The Westin Copley Place Boston Hotel, and then Boston Marriott Copley Place Hotel. To the left are Trinity Church and hotels. Storrow Drive is by Charles River

11.4. Infrastructure

- infrastructure improvement and maintenance at the world level

There is much need for good roads and bridges everywhere.

Italy, Venezia, Palazzi Fontana (left), Ca' D'Oro (center-right) and Sagredo (right), north bank, 550 m east of Ponte degli Scalzi.

11.5. Innovation, improvements

- innovation and improvements in all areas, at the world level
- Healthy environment for all people on Earth – no mosquitos, and elimination of all dangerous insects and animals.

There will be many more innovations and improvements, because all people will help each other.

Finland, Helsinki: The north-east of the Three smiths square, with the tram 7B on Aleksanterinkatu, the department store Stockmann (1930. right) and Tallberg's commerce house (left).

11.6. Transportation

- transportation at the world level
- safety
- security
- aviation
- highway
- cars
- railroads without noise
- maritime administration
- logistics

Electricity will be heavily used in all the forms of transportation.

At the north turn to right of Trinity Lane, a Trinity College (1546) gate, with the west part of the southern building (center right) of the Trinity College Great Court (the largest enclosed court in Europe).

11.7. Strategic planning

- strategic planning at the world level
- public works
- fleet maintenance

Good leadership needs reliable strategic planning.

Piazza Venezia and Altare della Patria or Il Monumento Nazionale (1911 -1925) a Vittorio Emanuele II, with Christmas decorations.

11.8. Standards

- standards: weights, measures, etc.
- The Standard of Weights and Measures will be the current International Standards.

Standards are needed in all engineering projects, to be easy for all on the planet.

USA, New York: on W 34th St, Empire State Building (center back), Snoopy second on left, looking southeast: on left a letter from the Postmaster.

11.9. Scientific & technical research

- research at the world level
- risk analysis
- laboratories
- engineering
- AI technologies make it possible to get rid of the inertia and slowness of the old bureaucratic machine, and to radically increase transparency and efficiency of administrative procedures. AI has capabilities to solve the problems of each person, and ultimately to change the quality of the entire system of world public administration. AI can help to have comfortable and safe cities, accessible and high-quality healthcare and education, modern logistics and a reliable transportation system, exploration of space and the world ocean, sustainable and balanced development, the growing quality of life and new opportunities for people.

Sunset on the Tyrrhenian Sea, in Fregene, near the Fiumicino Airport, 25 km west of Rome.

11.10. Communications

- communications at the world level
- telecommunications
- networks
- the phone companies must eliminate all phone-criminals before they steal people's money – they will pay a police unit to help them, if necessary.

UK, Oxford: A Public Library close to Christ Church College (1546) and Merton College (1264, named after Walter de Merton).

11.11. Peaceful nuclear energy use

- peaceful nuclear energy use at the world level
- safety
- waste
- electrical power

The nuclear energy is essential, and it will be used only for peaceful purposes.

USA, Cambridge, 1 Feb 2010, on Massachusetts Avenue, looking northeast to the west façade of the Department of Urban Studies and Planning (left), and the main entrance to the Massachusetts Institute of Technology (MIT, 1861, center).

11.12. Oceanic analysis

- oceanic analysis at the world level
- All the oceans will belong to some of the regions defined before, therefore will be maintained by those regions, to be free of any piracy or other bad activity – World Police will help when necessary.

Piazza Venezia and Altare della Patria or Il Monumento Nazionale (1911 -1925) a Vittorio Emanuele II, with Christmas decorations.

11.13. Atmospheric analysis

- atmospheric analysis at the global level
- meteorological service and prognosis at the global level

Prevention of bad atmospheric event is possible, and will be done at global level.

From Clare Bridge (1640, 1969) over River Cam, looking north to the Garret Hostel Bridge (center back), Punting Cambridge (center right), Trinity Hall Garden (right), Clare Fellows Garden (left).

11.14. Non-bureaucratic world resources use

- world resources analysis
- sustainable use of these resources
- geographical and geological activity

UK, Cambridge, a bas-relief on the eastern wall of the western building of the Old Court (1451) of Queens' College (1448), University of Cambridge, 60 m east of the Mathematical Bridge (1749).

11.15. Non-bureaucratic product safety

- product safety at the global level
- hazardous material and chemical safety

Rome: Accademia Nazionale dei Lincei (1603) in Villa Farnesina (1510). The author was invited to give a lecture here in 1978.

11.16. Broadcasting

- government broadcasting (radio, tv, Internet, newspaper, etc.) including news, scientific and technical information
- private broadcasting will continue, but the world government must be able to directly inform the people, without intermediaries
- responsible broadcasting is a necessity

USA, Boston, 16 April 2016, in the northwest corner of the Boston Public Garden, near Beacon St and Arlington St, the statue Angel of the Waters (1924 by Daniel Chester French) for George Robert White (1847 – 1922, prominent Boston businessman and philanthropist) Memorial.

11.17. Space exploration

- space exploration and expansion at the world level – very important for the future

There are now private companies, which participate with success in the space exploration projects.

Italy, Naples (Napoli 1500 BC), Castel Nuovo (1282, called Maschio Angioino), in front of Piazza Municipio and the city hall

11.18. Patent

- patent and trademark
- intellectual rights - The intellectual rights will be respected, based mostly on the current rules, managed by assistants

Sweden, Malmö, from Skeppsbron looking north to the north part of the west side of the Central Station (right), sign for Trelleborg and Limhamn (to left), Goteborg and Hamnen (straight).

11.19. Volunteers for this department

- In order to better know the world government, to help it, and, especially, to improve it, all able people of the world will work as volunteers at least one day/year in the local facility of this department, which will have a special office for managing this volunteer work.

UK, London: from the Abingdon St., looking northeast to the south (left, House of Commons) and west (right, House of Lords) façades of the Palace of Westminster (1016, 1870), with the Old Palace Yard, and the statue of the King Richard I of England (Coeur de Lion (the Lionheart), 1157-1199 (aged 42), King 1189-1199 (10 years), center).

12 – Level 3: 770,000,000 people

The 10 L3 friendly managers of the 10 regions, each with about 770,000,000 people, will daily discuss with, and practically assist, the 10 L2 managers of their 10 sub-regions, and will continuously work for improvements:

- must be much closer to the people – all managers, at all levels, will weekly randomly contact people and ask what is on their minds, and what they really need.

- each of the 10 L3 friendly managers of the 10 regions will receive 2.5% of the world taxes of, which are, let's say, 12 T coins (supposing that the new world currency coin will be close in value to the dollar) (GDP $85 T in 2018), therefore, let's say about 300,000,000,000 coins. This is a lot of money for a region, but if some regions want more, with the approval of the region's people, they can decide to have a region tax.

- At least 30% of the money will be sent to villages and cities.

- All the budgets based on these taxes must have a 2% surplus.

- At the meridians which separate the regions will not be any restrictions, how is now between different regions of a country.

12.1. 10 regions

Let's remember the new 10 regions, called R0, R1,..., R9, which will be delimited (for easier administration) by meridians (or line of longitudes), with the assistance of the United Nations, each region having a pair of capitals (which will change every year), for example:

R0 between meridians 0 and 15^0 E, capitals: Bern and Libreville (Gabon)

R1: 15^0 E - 30^0 E, Warsaw (Poland) and Pretoria (South Africa)

R2: 30^0 E - 45^0 E, Moscow and Cairo

R3: 45^0 E - 75^0 E, Astana (Kazakhstan) and Karachi (Pakistan)

R4: 75^0 E - 85^0 E, New Delhi (India) and Tomsk (Russia)

R5: 85^0 E - 100^0 E, Kuala Lumpur (Malaysia) and Quanzhou (China)

R6: 100^0 E - 115^0 E, Jakarta (Indonesia) and Beijing

R7: 115^0 E - 180^0, Tokyo and Sydney (Australia)

R8: 180^0 - 70^0 W, Washington and Mexico City

R9: 70^0 W – 0, Halifax (Canada) and Brasilia

12.2. Non-bureaucratic region Government

Like the World Government, the Region Governments are limited to a Region Manager Office (less than 8 people), and 7 small departments – they take the general rules and decisions from the world government, and implement and adapt them at the region level:

12.2.1 – Region Tax – helps to collect taxes and to assist taxpayers.

12.2.2 – Region Treasury – helps the world treasury at the region level, creates regions' budgets, and manages regions' finances

12.2.3 – Region People Assistance - helps the world People Assistance at the region level

The same for the other region departments:

12.2.4 – Region Medical

12.2.5 – Region Police

12.2.6 – Region Education

12.2.7 – Region Science & Technology

- Constant attention will be focused on avoiding duplication at all levels of the world government – there must be continuous collaboration between all levels, to prevent duplication and to eliminate it, if it was found.

13 – Level 2: 77,000,000 people

The 100 L2 friendly managers of the 100 sub-regions, each with about 77,000,000 people, will daily discuss with, and practically assist the 10 L1 managers, of their 10 districts, and will continuously work for improvements.

Rome: Piazza Venezia from Altare della Patria, Palazzo Venezia (1455

13.1. Much closer to the people, no bureaucracy

- must be much closer to the people– all managers, at all levels, will weekly randomly contact people and ask what is on their minds, and what they really need.
- each of the 100 L2 friendly managers of the 100 sub-regions will receive 0.25% of the world taxes of, which are, let's say, 12 T coins (supposing that the new world currency coin will be close in value to the dollar) (GDP $85 T in 2018), therefore, let's say about 30,000,000,000 coins. This is a lot of money for a sub-region, but if some sub-regions want more, with the approval of the sub-region's people, they can decide to have a sub-region tax.
- At least 40% of the money will be sent to villages and cities.
- All the budgets based on these taxes must have a 2% surplus.
- We remember that each region will be divided by meridians in 10 sub-regions S00,   , S99, each with about 77 M people.

UK, London: on Newington Butts St., looking northwest to Metropolitan Tabernacle (1650, left), and London College of Communication.

13.2 Non-bureaucratic Sub-Region Government

Like the World Government, and the Region Governments, the Sub-Region Government are limited to a Sub-Region Manager Office (less than 6 people), and 7 small departments – they take the general rules and decisions from the world and region governments, and implement and adapt them at the sub-region level:

13.2.1 – Sub-Region Tax – helps to collect taxes and to assist taxpayers.

13.2.2 – Sub-Region Treasury – helps at the sub-region level, creates sub-regions' budgets, and manages sub-regions' finances

13.2.3 – Sub-Region People Assistance - helps at the sub-region level

The same for the other sub-region departments:

13.2.4 – Sub-Region Medical

13.2.5 – Sub-Region Police

13.2.6 – Sub-Region Education

13.2.7 – Sub-Region Science & Technology

- Constant attention will be focused on avoiding duplication at all levels of the world government – there must be continuous collaboration between all levels, to prevent duplication and to eliminate it, if it was found.

14 – Level 1: 7,800,000 people

The 1,000 L1 friendly managers of the 1,000 districts, each with about 7,800,000 people, will daily discuss with and practically assist the mayors and town managers from their districts, and will continuously work for improvements.

Rome: Trajan's Market, which is the north-est part of Forum Traiani (113)

14.1. Really closer to the people and no bureaucracy

- must be much closer to the people - all managers, at all levels, will weekly randomly contact people and ask what is on their minds, and what they really need.

- each of the 1,000 L1 friendly managers of the 1,000 districts will receive 0.025% of the world taxes of, which are, let's say, 12 T coins (supposing that the new world currency coin will be close in value to the dollar) (GDP $85 T in 2018), therefore, let's say about 3,000,000,000 coins. This is a lot of money for a district, but if some districts want more, with the approval of the district's people, they can decide to have a local tax, or sales tax, or value added tax, etc.

- At least 50% of the money will be sent to villages and cities.

- All the budgets based on these taxes must have a 2% surplus.

France, Paris: From L'Église de la Madeleine (1842) – Rue Royale, the Egyptian obelisk (circa 1250 BC) in Place de la Concord (1772), and Palais Bourbon (1728, Napoleon 1806), now for l'Assemblée Nationale.

14.2 Non-bureaucratic District Government

Like the World Government, the Region Governments, and the Sub-Region Government, the District Governments are limited to a District Manager Office (less than 4 people), and 7 small departments – they take the general rules and decisions from the world, region and sub-region governments, and implement and adapt them at the district level:

14.2.1 – District Tax – helps to collect taxes and to assist taxpayers.

14.2.2 – District Treasury – helps at the district level, creates districts' budgets, and manages districts' finances

14.2.3 – District People Assistance - helps at the district level

The same for the other district departments:

14.2.4 – District Medical

14.2.5 – District Police

14.2.6 – District Education

14.2.7 – District Science & Technology

14.3. Local level with no bureaucracy

- The local level managers – mayors, town managers, county managers – are the closest to the people, and must be permanently assisted, and asked how the work is going.
- They will report to the district managers how they used the money which they received from the district, sub-region, region and the world management
- A daily dialog will be with all the other levels managers, to make sure that they receive what they need.

The south-west side of the Amphitheatrum Flavium (Colosseum, 80 AD), with a flag throwing festival on December 8, 2011.

14.4. No duplication, no bureaucracy

- Constant attention will be focused on avoiding duplication at all levels of the world government – there must be continuous collaboration between all levels, to prevent duplication and to eliminate it, if it was found.

UK, Cambridge, a bas-relief on the eastern wall of the western building of the Old Court (1451) of Queens' College (1448), University of Cambridge, 60 m east of the Mathematical Bridge (1749).

15 – World Constitution

The following are the main World Constitution subjects (please see the book The Constitution of the World):

- rules
- small World Government, with 7 small departments
- elections - every 20 months for one term only, based on exceptional results, no propaganda
- advisors' levels - minimum age 25 years, First Adviser for one month, by rotation
- assistants
- administrators
- Honorific Word Observer
- medical assistance, Specialized Medical Institutions for disorderly behavior
- people assistance services
- some police with small arms
- total disarmament
- no conflicts
- no war
- no military forces
- no arms
- no abuses
- freedom and responsibility
- people can assemble peacefully only
- census: A census will take place every 5 years – starting, let's say on October 1st, 2023 - and all the people will receive a special credit card (SCC), with their photo and other personal data.
- special credit card with photo and other personal data. The special credit card (SCC) will be used to buy everything, to identify for voting, for census, for travel, for medical assistance, etc.
- World Central Bank: The SCC will be issued by the World Central Bank, which will include all current central banks – starting, let's say on May 1st, 2023.
- new world currency

- budgets with surplus
- tax: 15% of income
- no borrowing
- 40 hours/week, compensation
- savings accounts for old age
- International standards
- Intellectual Property
- World Post Offices
- free commerce and collaboration
- common sense
- prevention of bad events first - if bad, then pay all expense and reimburse
- language and alphabet

Italia, Venezia, Palazzi Ca' D'Oro (center-right) and Sagredo (right), north bank, 570 m east of Ponte degli Scalzi.

16 - Conclusions

- It is obvious that if all aver 2 B of children on Earth will get a solid education (see my book at number 90 in bibliography: Our Future Depends on Good World Educations – Moving from frail education to solid education), our future will be in good hands!

- The purpose of education is to give a solid foundation for a good life.

- The purpose for all over 7.7 B of people on Earth is to be healthy, to live in peace, freedom and harmony, to be prosperous, and to prepare to expand to the Moon, asteroids, Mars, and other places in the Universe, which can support life.

Ideas for the future, having a good World Government, as described in this book:

- Reserve time for happiness
- In general, people should use robots and automated processes, work less, and spend more time with their families
- The weekend should be like a small vacation
- Prevent burnout
- Make compassion an important issue
- Eliminate stress
- Help colleagues
- Perfectionism is an objective which cannot be achieved, but try to come as close to it as possible.

Without bureaucracy the world will be much better, and the people much happier!

Therefore, eliminate bureaucracy and keep it away!

France, Paris: La Monnaie de Paris (the Direction of Coins and Medals) created in 864 by Charles II (823-877, king 843-877), is the oldest French institution, which is still active. It also has a Musée de la Monnaie (1833), at 11 Quai de Conti, in the 6th arrondissement.

Bibliography

"The Histories" by Polybius

"Discours de la Méthode" by René Descartes

"Meditationes de prima philosophia" by René Descartes

"Philosophiae Naturalis Principia Mathematica" by Isaac Newton

Chinese encyclopedia Gujin Tushu Jicheng (Imperial Enciclopaedia)

"Encyclopédie" by Jean-Baptiste le Rond d'Alembert and Denis Diderot

"Encyclopaedia Britannica" by over 4,400 contributors

"Encyclopedia Americana" by Francis Lieber

"Grand Larousse encyclopédique en 24 volumes" by Albert Ducrocq

Nobel Prize Organization

"The Cambridge History of Medicine", edited by Roy Porter

"Great Russian Encyclopedia" by Yury Osipov

"Encyclopedia of China"

"Enciclopedia Italiana di Scienze, Lettere ed Arti" (35 volume), by Giovanni Treccani

Concise Oxford Dictionary of Opera

"Allgemeine Encyclopädie der Wissenschaften und Künste" by Johann Samuel Ersch und Johann Gottfried Gruber

Grove Dictionary of Music and Musicians

"Gran Enciclopedia de España"

Other sources include: UPI, CNBC, AP, Nasdaq, Reuters, EDGAR, AFP, Recode, Europa Press, Bloomberg News, Fox News, USA, Deutsche Presse-Agentur, MSNBC, BBC, American Mathematical Society, Mathematical Reviews, Australian Associated Press, Agência Brasil, The Canadian Press (La Presse Canadienne), Middle East News Agency, Baltic News Service, Suomen Tietotoimisto, Athens-Macedonian News Agency, Asian News International, Inter Press Service, Kyodo News, Notimex, Algemeen Nederlands Persbureau, AGERPRES, Newsis, Tidningarnas Telegrambyrå, Swiss Telegraphic Agency, Central News Agency, ANKA news agency, Agenzia Fides

UK, Oxford, from the Logic Ln, looking north to the High St and the south gate of the Queen's College (1341, founded by Robert de Eglesfield (1295-1349, chaplain of the Queen consort) in honor of Queen consort Philippa of Hainault (1314-1369, wife of Edward III of England (1312-1377, Reign 1327-1377, burial Westminster Abbey, they had 13 children, and their great-grandfather was King Philip III of France (1245-1285, reign 1270-1285))), University College (1249, left).

Michael M. Dediu is also the author of these books (which can be found on Amazon.com):

1. Aphorisms and quotations – with examples and explanations
2. Axioms, aphorisms and quotations – with examples and explanations
3. 100 Great Personalities and their Quotations
4. Professor Petre P. Teodorescu – A Great Mathematician and Engineer
5. Professor Ioan Goia – A Dedicated Engineering Professor
6. Venice (Venezia) – a new perspective. A short presentation with photographs
7. La Serenissima (Venice) - a new photographic perspective. A short presentation with many photos
8. Grand Canal – Venice. A new photographic viewpoint. A short presentation with many photos
9. Piazza San Marco – Venice. A different photographic view. A short presentation with many photos
10. Roma (Rome) - La Città Eterna. A new photographic view. A short presentation with many photos
11. Why is Rome so Fascinating? A short presentation with many photos
12. Rome, Boston and Helsinki. A short photographic presentation
13. Rome and Tokyo – two captivating cities. A short photographic presentation
14. Beautiful Places on Earth – A new photographic presentation
15. From Niagara Falls to Mount Fuji via Rome - A novel photographic presentation
16. From the USA and Canada to Italy and Japan - A fresh photographic presentation
17. Paris – Why So Many Call This City Mon Amour - A lovely photographic presentation
18. The City of Light – Paris (La Ville-Lumière) - A kaleidoscopic photographic presentation
19. Paris (Lutetia Parisiorum) – the romance capital of the world - A kaleidoscopic photographic view
20. Paris and Tokyo – a joyful photographic presentation. With a preamble about the Universe

From the northeast corner of Trafalgar Square, south of the National Gallery, looking southwest to Vice Admiral Horatio Nelson's (1758-1805 (aged 47), buried at St Paul's Cathedral) Column, and the equestrian statue of King George IV (1762-1830 (aged 68), King 1820-1830, patron of architecture, the eldest son of King George III (1738-1820 (aged 81), Reign 1760-1820 (59 years), during his reign, the American colonies created the U. S. A.)).

21. From USA to Japan via Canada – A cheerful photographic documentary

22. 200 Wonderful Places, In The Last 50 Years – A personal photographic documentary

23. Must see places in USA and Japan - A kaleidoscopic photographic documentary

24. Grandeurs of the World - A kaleidoscopic photographic documentary

25. Corneliu Leu – writer on the same wavelength as Mark Twain. An American viewpoint

26. From Berkeley to Pompeii via Rome – A kaleidoscopic photographic documentary

27. From America to Europe via Japan - A kaleidoscopic photographic documentary

28. Discover America and Japan - A photographic documentary

29. J. R. Lucas – philosopher on a creative parallel with Plato, An American viewpoint

30. From America to Switzerland via France - A photographic documentary

31. From Bretton Woods to New York via Cape Cod - A photographic documentary

32. Splendid Places on the Atlantic Coast of the U. S. A. - A photographic documentary

33. Fourteen nice Cities on three Continents - A photographic documentary

34. 17 Picturesque Cities on the World Map - A photographic documentary

35. Unforgettable Places from Four Continents including Trump buildings - A photographic documentary

36. Dediu Newsletter, Volume 1, Number 1, 6 December 2016 – Monthly news, review, comments and suggestions for a better and wiser world

37. Dediu Newsletter, Volume 1, Number 2, 6 January 2017 (available at www.derc.com).

38. Dediu Newsletter, Volume 1, Number 3, 6 February 2017 (available at www.derc.com).

39. London and Greenwich, A photographic documentary

From Trinity Ln, looking west through the entrance of Trinity Hall, (1350, by William Baterman (c 1298-1355, Bishop of Norwich between 1344 and 1355), a constituent college (the 5th oldest) of the University of Cambridge), to the Front Court and the entrance to the west building of the Front Court. To the northeast of Trinity Hall there is the separate Trinity College (1546, founder Henry VIII (1491-1547, reign 1509-1547), motto: Virtus Vera Nobilitas

40. Dediu Newsletter, Volume 1, Number 4, 6 March 2017 (available also at www.derc.com).

41. Dediu Newsletter, Volume 1, Number 5, 6 April 2017 (available also at www.derc.com).

42. Dediu Newsletter, Volume 1, Number 6, 6 May 2017 (available also at www.derc.com).

43. Dediu Newsletter, Volume 1, Number 7, 6 June 2017 (available also at www.derc.com).

44. London, Oxford and Cambridge, A photographic documentary

45. Dediu Newsletter, Volume 1, Number 8, 6 July 2017 (available also at www.derc.com).

46. Dediu Newsletter, Volume 1, Number 9, 6 August 2017 (available also at www.derc.com).

47. Dediu Newsletter, Volume 1, Number 10, 6 September 2017 (available also at www.derc.com).

48. Three Great Professors: President Woodrow Wilson, Historian Germán Arciniegas, Mathematician Gheorghe Vrănceanu, A chronological and photographic documentary

49. Dediu Newsletter, Volume 1, Number 11, 6 October 2017 (available also at www.derc.com).

50 Dediu Newsletter, Volume 1, Number 12, 6 November 2017 (available also at www.derc.com).

51 Dediu Newsletter, Volume 2, Number 1 (13), 6 December 2017 (available also at www.derc.com).

52 Two Great Leaders: Augustus and George Washington, A chronological and photographic documentary

53. Dediu Newsletter, Volume 2, Number 2 (14), 6 January 2018 (available also at www.derc.com).

54. Newton, Benjamin Franklin, and Gauss, A chronological and photographic documentary

55. Dediu Newsletter, Volume 2, Number 3 (15), 6 February 2018 (available also at www.derc.com).

56. 2017: World Top Events, But Many Little Known, A chronological and photographic documentary

57. Dediu Newsletter, Volume 2, Number 4 (16), 6 March 2018 (available also at www.derc.com).

58. Vergilius, Horatius, Ovidius, and Shakespeare, A chronological and photographic documentary.

From Trinity Lane looking southeast to the west façade with the entrance to the Old Schools (1441, University Offices, the administrative center of the university, surrounded to the north by Gonville and Caius College (1348), to the east by the University of Cambridge Senate House (1722, where degree ceremonies are held, on King's Parade), to the south by the King's College Chapel (1446), and to the west by Trinity Hall (1350) and Clare College (1326)).

59. Dediu Newsletter, Volume 2, Number 5 (17), 6 April 2018 (available also at www.derc.com).

60. Dediu Newsletter, Volume 2, Number 6 (18), 6 May 2018 (available also at www.derc.com).

61. Vivaldi, Bach, Mozart, and Verdi, A chronological and photographic documentary

62. Dediu Newsletter, Volume 2, Number 7 (19), 6 June 2018 (available also at www.derc.com).

63. Dediu Newsletter, Volume 2, Number 8 (20), 6 July 2018 (available also at www.derc.com).

64. Dediu Newsletter, Volume 2, Number 9 (21), 6 August 2018 (available also at www.derc.com).

65. World History, a new perspective - A chronological and photographic documentary.

66. World Humor History with over 100 Jokes, a new perspective - A chronological and photographic documentary

67. Dediu Newsletter, Vol 2, N 10 (22), 6 September 2018

68. Dediu Newsletter, Vol 2, N 11 (23), 6 October 2018

69. Da Vinci, Michelangelo, Rembrandt, Rodin - A chronological and photographic documentary

70. Dediu Newsletter, Vol 2, N 12 (24), 6 November 2018

71. Dediu Newsletter, Vol 3, N 1 (25), 6 December 2018

72. From Euclid to Edison - revelries in the last 75 years - A chronological and photographic documentary

73. Dediu Newsletter, Vol 3, N 2 (26), 6 January 2019

74. Socrates to Churchill - Aphorisms celebrated after 1960 - A chronological and photographic documentary

75. Dediu Newsletter Vol 3, Number 3 (27), 6 February 2019

76. Hippocrates to Fleming: Medicine History celebrated after 1943 - A chronological and photographic documentary

77. Dediu Newsletter, Volume 3, Number 4 (28), 6 March 2019

78. Dediu Newsletter, Volume 3, Number 5 (29), 6 April 2019

79. Archimedes to Ford: Invention History celebrated after 1943 - A chronological and photographic documentary

80. Dediu Newsletter, Volume 3, Number 6 (30), 6 May 2019

81. Sutherland to Pavarotti: Great Singers History - A chronological and photographic documentary

82. Dediu Newsletter, Volume 3, Number 7 (31), 6 June 2019

83. Dediu Newsletter, Volume 3, Number 8 (32), 6 July 2019

Inside London Liverpool Street Station (1874, central London railway terminus, with an atrium ceiling, in the north-eastern corner of the City of London, in the ward of Bishopsgate), train to Cambridge (founded around 50 AD (the principal Roman site is a small fort (*castrum*) Duroliponte on Castle Hill, just northwest of the city center; it was constructed around AD 70 and converted to civilian use around 50 years later. Evidence of more widespread Roman settlement has been discovered including numerous farmsteads, and a village in the Cambridge district of Newnham. Following the Roman withdrawal from Britain around 410, the location may have been abandoned), a university city on the River Cam, area 41 km^2, population 125,000, elevation 6 m, in eastern England, 80 km northeast of London, 120 km northeast of Oxford, home to the prestigious University of Cambridge (1209), to the east there is Cambridge International Airport). University of Cambridge is formed from a variety of institutions which include 31 constituent colleges, and over 100 academic departments organized into six schools. Cambridge is the second-oldest university in the English-speaking world, and the world's third-oldest surviving university. The university grew out of an association of scholars who left the University of Oxford, after a dispute with the townspeople.

84. Augustus to Rockefeller: History of the Wealthiest People - A chronological and photographic documentary

85. Dediu Newsletter, Volume 3, Number 9 (33), 6 August 2019

86 – Pythagoras to Fermi: History of Science - A chronological and photographic documentary

87. Dediu Newsletter, Volume 3, Number 10 (34), 6 September 2019

88. Our Future is Sustainable Peace and Prosperity – Moving from conflicts to harmony and peace

89 - Dediu Newsletter, Volume 3, Number 11 (35), 6 October 2019 – World Monthly Report with News

90 – Our Future Depends on Good World Educations – Moving from frail education to solid education

91 - Dediu Newsletter, Volume 3, Number 12 (36), 6 November 2019 – World Monthly Report with News

92 – Friendly, Helpful & Smart World Management - Moving from bureaucracy to responsive world management

93 – If You Want Peace, Prepare for Peace! – Moving from preparation for war to preparation for peace

94 - Dediu Newsletter, Volume 4, Number 1 (37), 6 December 2019 – World Monthly Report with News and Suggestions for Sustainable Peace, Freedom and Prosperity

95 – World with One Country & its Ten Friendly Regions - Moving from 195 disagreeing countries, to 1 country with 10 collaborating regions

96 - Dediu Newsletter, Volume 4, Number 2 (38), 6 January 2020 – World Monthly Report with News and Suggestions for Sustainable Peace, Freedom and Prosperity

97 – After 10,000 Years of Conflicts, People want 10,000 Years of Harmony - Moving from continuous wars to stable peace

98 - Dediu Newsletter, Volume 4, Number 3 (39), 6 February 2020 – World Monthly Report with News and Suggestions for Sustainable Peace, Freedom and Prosperity

99 – The Constitution of the World – Moving from many unsustainable constitutions, to just one Constitution of the World

100 - Dediu Newsletter, Volume 4, Number 4 (40), 6 March 2020 – World Monthly Report with News and Suggestions for Sustainable Peace, Freedom and Prosperity

France, Paris, La Seine, on Parisis boat, looking upstream to the left bank, towards east: Port de Suffren with Vedettes de Paris Croisières (Cruises), near Quai Branly, the north-west and south-west sides of la Tour Eiffel (1889, 324 m, 279 m at the 3rd level observatory), with pilier north on the left, pilier est on the center left back, pilier vest on the center front, and pilier south on the right; the south-east end of Pont d'Iéna (1808-1814, named by Napoléon after his victory in 1806 at the Battle of Jena, 1937, 155 m by 35 m, left.

101 - Dediu Newsletter, Volume 4, Number 5 (41), 6 April 2020 – World Monthly Report

102 - Dediu Newsletter, Volume 4, Number 6 (42), 6 May 2020 – World Monthly Report

103 – World Constitution Implementation – Moving from violent changes, to smooth transition to the Constitution of the World

104 - Dediu Newsletter, Volume 4, Number 7 (43), 6 June 2020 – World Monthly Report

105 - Dediu Newsletter, Volume 4, Number 8 (44), 6 July 2020 – World Monthly Report

106 - It is getting truer and truer – we urgently need the World Constitution: Moving from anarchic changes, to balanced transition to the Constitution of the World

107 - Dediu Newsletter, Volume 4, Number 9 (45), 6 August 2020 – World Monthly Report

108 - World Constitution with Lovely Comments - Moving from many suboptimal constitutions to the much better Constitution of the World

109 - Dediu Newsletter, Volume 4, Number 10 (46), 6 September 2020 – World Monthly Report

110 – World Constitution with Questions & Answers – Moving from many obsolete constitutions to the much better Constitution of the World

111 - Dediu Newsletter, Volume 4, Number 11 (47), 6 October 2020 – World Monthly Report

112 - World Projects - Moving from minor projects to great projects for the World

113 - Dediu Newsletter, Volume 4, Number 12 (48), 6 November 2020 – World Monthly Report

114 - Dediu Newsletter, Volume 5, Number 1 (49), 6 December 2020 – World Monthly Report

115 - World Opportunities for All - Moving from few local jobs, to world opportunities for all

116 - Dediu Newsletter, Volume 5, Number 2 (50), 6 January 2021 – World Monthly Report

117 - Self-Managing World - Moving from local ruling top-down, to self-managing world

118 – We are all in the same space boat – Peaceful Terra; Moving from local fragile boats to the solid Peaceful Terra

119 - Dediu Newsletter, Volume 5, Number 3 (51), 6 February 2021 – World Monthly Report
120 - All people ask for Peace + Freedom = Prosperity, Moving from local conflicts to world peace and freedom
121 - Dediu Newsletter, Volume 5, Number 4 (52), 6 March 2021 – World Monthly Report
122 – To pour Peace from a cup full of arms, MELT ALL ARMS! – Moving from arms race, to peace enjoyment
123 - Dediu Newsletter, Volume 5, Number 5 (53), 6 April 2021 – World Monthly Report

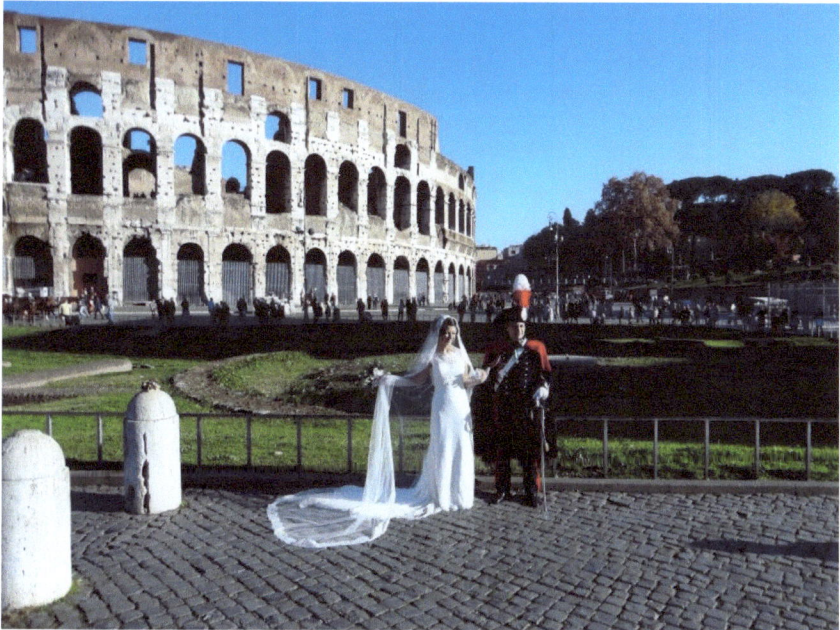

Rome: The south-west side of the Amphitheatrum Flavium (Colosseum, 80 AD) and a carabiniere wedding photo event.

www.ingramcontent.com/pod-product-compliance
Lightning Source LLC
Chambersburg PA
CBHW041308210326
41599CB00003B/31